TURNING MOURNING INTO DANCING

Adult Coloring Book

John I. Penn and Wanda Parker Rains

Scripture passages taken from:
All Scripture quotations, unless otherwise designated, are taken from the *New Revised Standard Version*, "NRSV," New Testament © 1989 by the Division of Christian Education of the National Council of the Churches of Christ in the U.S.A. Used by permission.

Scripture quotations marked "NKJV" are taken from the *New King James Version* ©, Copyright © 1982 Thomas Nelson, Inc. Used by permission. All rights reserved.

Scripture quotations marked "NLT" are taken from the Holy Bible, *New Living Translation.* © Copyright 1996, 2004, 2015. Used by permission of Tyndale House Publishers, Inc., Carol Stream, Illinois 60188. All rights reserved.

Scripture quotations marked "TLB" are taken from the *New Living Bible*, copyright ©1971. Tyndale House Publishers, Inc., P.O. Box 80, Wheaton, Illinois 60189. Used by permission. All rights reserved.

Cover Designed and Illustrations by Wanda Parker Rains
Interior Designed by John I. Penn
Photograph of John Penn on Back Cover by Stephen A. Penn

ISBN: 10: 0-9720785-6-8
ISBN :13: 978-0-9720785-6-6
Library of Congress-in-Publication Data

Penn, John I.

Spirituality, Well-being, Wholeness, Art, Creativity, Grief, Healing/John I. Penn and Wanda Parker Rains

This book is dedicated to my siblings—
Sophie, Gary, Jimmy, Carolyn, Barbara,
Charles, and Richard—
who are mourning the death of our mother,
Josephine Penn.

TABLE OF CONTENTS

TABLE OF CONTENT continued

FOREWORD

Many of us have heard the words: *"we all don't grieve the same"*. My mother used to say: *"the missing ever stops"*. When I was twelve years of age, I started keeping a diary, then as I grew older, a journal. Yet I had never experienced the calming effects or the impact of using different colors creatively and reducing my level of stress, until 2018 when I took with me on a cruise, my first adult coloring book, *Turning Mourning into Dancing* authored by the Rev. John I. Penn and illustrated by Wanda Parker Rains. Rev. Penn's commentary on various scriptures along with the illustrations, enabled me to release the pain and loss of the deaths of my father, Rev. Dr. Gloster B. Current (1997) former national executive with the NAACP, my husband, Rev. Dr. Robert E. "TEX" Felder (2006) United Methodist ordained elder for 45 years and my mother, Bishop Leontine Turpeau Current Kelly (2012), the first African American woman to be elected to the Episcopacy of the United Methodist Church (1984) and of any mainline denomination.

Turning Mourning into Dancing helped me to release the feeling of loneliness and celebrate the love that God had poured into me by and through my parents and my beloved husband. It also enabled me to appreciate that if we acknowledge God as our Lord and Savior, we realize that we do not walk through the valley alone and that God and our loved ones are always with us.
Upon return from the cruise, I purchased several copies of this unique coloring books for friends that had lost loved ones. Many of them shared that they had found it helpful as they journeyed through their valley of grief.

I am excited about this revised addition and look forward to using it and sharing with others.

Angella Current-Felder, Author
Breaking Barriers: An African American Family & the Methodist Story, Abingdon Press, 2001 and The School of Dreams in the Valley of Hope: The Africa University Story, Africa University Press, 2012.

INTRODUCTION

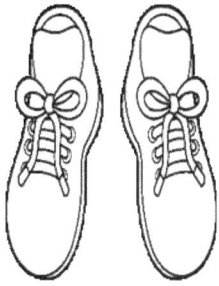

I have meticulously made significant revisions in *Turning Mourning into Dancing*. Each of the messages have been rewritten to improve the content and to be more thought-provoking. This book is written from a Christian perspective. It is designed as an adult coloring book. It is a collaboration with a long-time friend, Wanda Parker Rains. Wanda is a talented and gifted illustrator. This is our second book collaboration. I am delighted to include her unique illustrations in this resource!

People everywhere are discovering the wonderful benefits of coloring, such as reducing stress, managing depression, and a means of relaxing. The benefits of coloring are real and therapeutic. If you don't believe it, try it for yourself. Coloring is a stress buster. It can lower your anxiety and reduce your blood pressure.

On April 14, 2017, our ninety-three-year-old mother, Josephine Penn, transitioned to be with the Lord. My seven siblings are also mourning her death. Grieving mom's death has given me a new perspective on grief, loss, and the importance of doing the grief work well. My siblings, children, and grandchildren would agree that our grief over our mother's death was made easier because of the many years we had her in our lives.

Mother's death is the inspiration behind the concept and creation of this book. God knew what I needed to turn my sorrow into joy. God used my love of writing to meet much of my emotional, mental, and spiritual needs. The Holy Spirit guided me in the writing of the seventeen grief-related messages included in this book. Although this book is personal, it is designed for all who mourn to bring healing and therapeutic benefits, ultimately turning mourning into dancing.

In the book, I included the word "playful" intentionally. In Proverbs 17:22, King Solomon reminds us of the therapeutic value of a cheerful or joyful heart: "*A joyful heart is a good medicine, but a broken spirit drains one's strength.*" Each message and illustration are intended to offer you a creative and therapeutic tool, allowing you to have fun and play amid your loss and pain as you move through the grief process. Writing them has helped to heal and to turn my mourning into dancing.

Psychologist Nikki Martinez, Psy.D., LCPC, in her article, "7 Reasons Adult Coloring Books Are Great for Your Mental, Emotional, and Intellectual Health," points out that adult coloring books offer therapeutic benefits. Further, Martinez states that coloring is an alternative to meditation, both a means of relaxation and a calming tool. Coloring allows you to use both the right and left hemispheres of the brain. Coloring allows you to get in touch with the inner child that recalls happier times when you experienced less responsibility and stress.[1]

It is also essential to understand that a significant loss may be a death, a divorce, the loss of a job, or a broken relationship. We bring out several facts related to grief and stress in the book, primarily that grief is common to most people. People grieve differently and to different degrees. The more we have loved, the more we grieve. To heal, we must grieve well.

The illustrations and messages in this resource are unique to most adult coloring books. The coloring activities and the messages are designed to help you grieve well. They are intended to challenge growth and healing. As stated above, coloring is a fun way to relax. Enter that quiet place within, and carve out time to do something good for yourself. Coloring allows you to get away from the hustle and bustle of the daily stresses of life.

You owe it to yourself to live a stress-free life as much as possible. The activity of coloring allows you to get in touch with your inner conflict of pain and loss, giving yourself permission to play and tap into your creativity.

The Bible reminds us that sorrow doesn't always last. The psalmist confirms the idea that God's favor can transform sorrow into joy: "*Weeping may endure for a night, but joy comes in the morning*" (Ps. 30:5b NKJV).

This book is "not" for those suffering from clinical depression. If you are suffering from long-term stress or depression, you should seek help from your personal physician.

I hope that this adult coloring book will do for you, what it has done for me, turning your sorrows into joy and set your feet, as well as your soul, dancing. It is also dedicated to all those who mourn.

HOW TO USE THIS BOOK

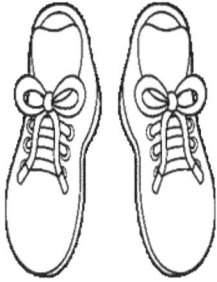

How you use this book is up to you. This coloring book is designed to encourage fun and play as a creative way to declutter the mind and relax the body, and help you embrace your current reality as you grieve the loss in your life. Each message included in this book is intended to inform and remind you of the resources you have—in God, in yourself, and others—to help you grow and heal.

This book has the potential to change your life for the better. As you use this unique coloring book, we encourage you to work through the book. As you color the illustrations, you can use crayons, watercolors, colored markers, or colored pencils.

We hope this book will remind you that you are loved, and that you are important. Even amid your pain and loss, God's grace is available to help you discover a new purpose as you move from uncertainty to a confident, meaningful life.

We have provided space in the book for you to journal your reflections, write down your discoveries, get in touch with your feelings and emotions, or record your growth and healing. You can also use this space to express your emotions and feelings through drawing, or composing a poem.

You may decide to use this coloring book as part of a small grief support group for persons who may be grieving alone. If your church does not have an active grief program, ask your pastor to consider starting one, using this adult coloring book on grief and loss.

As you get started, turn off your phone, computer, and TV. Although the content in this coloring book is designed in a certain way, you are free to choose a drawing and message that appeals to you on any given day. This is not a textbook. Carve out some quality time, and take your mind off everything except yourself, your wellness, and your God. Put on some uplifting and relaxing music. Relax, let go, and dance, dance, dance!

Your feedback and suggestions of your experience of this book will be greatly appreciated. Please share how this book might have helped or blessed you. You can communicate directly with the author via this email address below: *ministry652@gmial.com.*

Thank you for purchasing our book, and please share it with your friends and family. May the Lord, Jesus Christ, bless and keep you in perfect peace!

TURNING MOURNING INTO DANCING

This adult coloring book is a playful, healing, and inspirational book for those who have experienced the death of a loved one, a friend, a special acquaintance, or even a pet. Every significant loss is important, which may cause a person to grieve. Death is perhaps the loss that affects us most deeply and takes the most time to accept and heal. I know this personally.

In 1998, Jacqueline, our third child, died of cancer. At the age of thirty-three, she left behind three young children. When she died, I was away from home, teaching healing and wholeness in Sao Paulo, Brazil. One of the topics taught was related to death and grief. Through this experience, I discovered the importance of grace and the community of faith. God's healing power and grace are experienced best within the context of community, assuring that we are to be cared for and made whole again. No one should grieve alone!

In life, you are not on this journey alone. God is near to the brokenhearted. He knows pain and loss from the death of His Son. Remember, God sacrificed His only beloved Son to take away our sorrow and pain: "Surely he has borne our infirmities and carried our diseases" (Isa. 53:4). The only person that God loved yet turned away from was Jesus, who died, to take away the sins of the world. By turning away from His Son, as he was dying on a cross, God turned toward His broken and hurting humanity. When you and I hurt, God hurts also. God wants you to be whole. For this reason, he sacrificed his Son.

With God in your life, your mourning can genuinely turn into dancing. Think of healing, wholeness, and salvation as dancing. When you put your losses and hurts into God's compassionate hands, God's healing and comfort will lead you to dance both inwardly and outwardly.

Let this coloring book bring encouragement as you tap into your creativity. May your participation give you wings to soar above your situation and find release from the weight of your pain and loss. As you soar, you will see your situation from a new perspective, with everything appearing smaller. This unique perspective allows you to see through the Creator's eyes, who sees everything differently and holistically.

As you color, allow God to shoulder your burden, pain, and loss. God's shoulders are broad and strong. God can and will lighten your load. The messages and the drawings included in this book have been chosen to give you hope, peace, and joy. They are intended to facilitate growth and healing and create a merry heart—turning your mourning into dancing.

GOD WANTS TO BE CLOSE TO YOU

Revelation 3:14-22

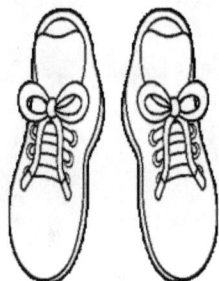

God wants to be a part of your life. God stands at the door of your heart, knocking and waiting for you to welcome Him in. You may try going through life alone, confused and depressed because you think God does not care about the difficult things you face day-to-day. The more complex life becomes, the more distant God appears to be. Nothing is further from the truth. Read the words of John the Revelator as he reveals the heart of God toward you:

"Behold, I stand at the door and knock. If anyone hears My voice and opens the door, I will come into him and dine with him, and he with Me. To him who overcomes I will grant to sit with Me on My throne, as I also overcame and sat down with My Father on His throne" (Revelation 3:20-21 *NKJV*).

God cares about every aspect of your life. He is waiting for you to welcome him into your life. He stands at the door, knocking and waiting for you to put out the welcome mat. God proved his great love by allowing His Son, Jesus, to suffer and die on the cross to remove every barrier Satan puts up to keep us apart.

You may leave God out of the most critical areas of your life. This may be especially true, even when you need divine wisdom and guidance, which could turn your mourning into dancing. If God cares for the birds of the air and the grasses of the field, how much more will God take care of you. You and I are much more valuable than either birds or grasses. God wants to be a father to you. God wants you to succeed and experience the abundant life Jesus Christ came to give. Open wide your heart and your mind to God, allowing Him access to your life. There is nothing God will not do for those who love and obey Him.

Remember, God created you for Himself to fulfill His destiny for your life. You were created for intimacy with the Living God. Jesus' death on the cross removed every barrier and obstacle that stands between you and God. Salvation is not about a set of rules of dos and don'ts; it's about pursuing a personal relationship with your Creator. God wants you to share in the oneness that He shares with His Son, Jesus Christ. Life is fuller and richer with God. God is the source of your physical, emotional, and spiritual well-being. How special is that?

God invites you to sit and eat with Him (John 3:20). In fact, through the cross, God is preparing you to sit with Christ on His throne. It is true; God loves you that much. Jesus even calls you a friend. You may put up walls between yourself and God because you misunderstand your true relationship with God. You may fear closeness with God because you don't think you measure up to His standards. And, on your own, you don't. God loves you for you. God accepts you just the way you are, and that may scare you. That's okay. Most people feel that way.

Here is the crux of the matter. You were created for continuous communion with God. God wants you to experience this authentic life here on earth, as His Son did. God sent the Holy Spirit to help you move closer and closer to God. When this life on earth is over, and if you have accepted God's redemptive grace, you will spend eternity with God. Open yourself to the God who loves you unconditionally. God is knocking on the door! Only you can open the door and let Him in.

REFLECTION

IN YOUR PRESENCE

In your presence, Lord, there is peace,

In your presence, Lord, there is hope,

In your presence, Lord, there is holiness,

In your presence, Lord, there is joy.

In your presence, Lord, let us come

In your presence, Lord, be as one,

In your presence, Lord, let our souls be touched.

Fill us with your Spirit and love.

From You alone comes our righteousness,

From You alone comes our holiness,

From You alone comes our peace and rest,

Through You, 0 Lord, we find love.

In your presence, Lord, we are made whole and complete.

In your presence, Lord, there is no fear or defeat,

In your presence, Lord, is my desire to be,

You give your love so rich and free.

In your presence, Lord, we abide.[2]

REFLECTIONS

A NEW SEASON

Throughout our lives, there are many seasons.
Some mixed with jubilation, sorrow and pain.
Some days are filled with blue skies and sunshine,
While others usher in dark clouds and rain.
But behind those clouds and darkened skies,
The sun is faithfully shining.
Often, we can't see it with our eyes,
Especially when our hearts are pining.
From the time we were born until the day we die,
Our journey is never complete
Until we cross the bridge of acceptance
That difficulty we will surely meet.
But the Word tells us very clearly
That every activity under heaven has a season.
Quite often there are valleys to be walked,
But for every one of them there is a reason.
What words of comfort we can offer you,
That new season is already drawing.
As you move from those unpleasant appointments
To a place of peace that comes in the morning.
This peace spoken of surpasses all imagined
And can never be quite understood.
It comes from our caring and merciful Father,
Given freely like none other could.
So, tonight feel God's loving presence
Manifested in this very room
And know you are moving from a season of uncertainty
To God's perfect peace where there is no gloom.[3]

REFLECTIONS

HOPE AND A FUTURE

Jeremiah 29:11

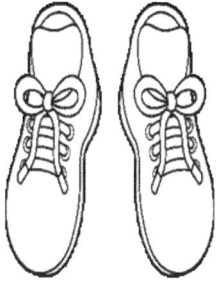

Whatever you are going through, or whatever situation life brings your way, God has a bright future for you. What matters is that you and God are on the same page. Life is uncertain and complex. Things don't always line up in your favor, but when you put your trust in God, He will give you a way out.

Life's uncertainties are not there to trip you up or to defeat you, but to make you stronger. If you love God and are living to please Him, God will turn your troubles into victories, your sorrows into joy. God steps in to protect His children, and He makes sure what you are created for will be accomplished. Your future is God's future. Your success reflects on God. Therefore, you must strive to discover God's purpose for your life.

Your future is already settled in heaven. Your goal is to make sure the kingdom work God has called you to do is carried out on earth. Your mission on earth, as Jesus puts it, is to be about your Father's business. When you are about your Father's business, your Father is about your business. Why? Because they are two sides of the same coin.

In the New Testament, Paul says, *"God works all things together for the good of those who love him, who have been called according to his purpose"* (Rom. 8:28 NIV). Jeremiah's words in the Old Testament give comfort, knowing that. God's plan is to bring blessings to his covenant people through both judgment and salvation; the two sides of the same coin. *"For I know the plans I have for you, declares the Lord, 'plans to prosper you and not to harm you, plans to give you hope and a future"* (Jer. 29:11 NIV).

God created you and me to do his kingdom work on earth. We are God's hands, feet, and voice. We are not just the King's kids; we are the King's workmanship, created to do good works. Followers of Jesus have been given the ministry task of sharing in God's kingdom work on earth, which God has predestined in heaven for us to do. Jesus even includes this critical fact in the prayer he taught his disciples: *"Thy will be done, on earth, as it is in heaven"* (Matt. 6:10 NIV).

Therefore, you can work through your grief and loss with hope because God has a plan for your future. God's plans are never to harm or hurt us. God's plans are "to prosper...and to give you hope and a future." Now, that should make you want to dance!

REFLECTIONS

COMMON TO ALL

1 Corinthians 10:13

Paul writes that no temptation will come to you that is not common to all. Paul states: *"No testing has overtaken you that is not common to everyone. God is faithful, and he will not let you be tested beyond your strength, but with the testing, he will also provide the way out so that you may be able to endure it"* (1 Corinthians 10:13 NRSV). Temptation is universal.

The apostle Paul makes the point that being tempted is not a sin. First, the temptation becomes a sin only when a person yields to it. Second, people throughout human history have resisted temptation. So, can you. Third, God is ready and willing to provide the strength and grace to resist and win over temptation. God is faithful and will not let you be tempted beyond your ability to resist. Fourth, God's resources of power and grace are always available to aid you in your time of need.

Finally, Paul offers assurance that when you hang in there and don't throw in the towel, the miracle happens despite the consequences of the temptation or testing. When you move through pain and sorrow, trusting in God's divine presence and grace, you will experience unspeakable joy. Why? Because you will know it is only by the grace of God that you were able to get through such an experience victoriously. Jesus confirms this to his disciples and you: *"I will never leave you nor forsake you"* (Heb. 13:5).

This means that Jesus Christ will be with us whether we are in the valley of pain and loss, and even death, or on the mountain top. It's dancing time!

REFLECTIONS

You are loved!

LEARNING TO COPE

Scripture

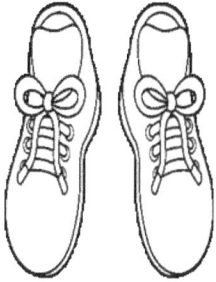

No one should have to grieve alone. Healing happens best within the faith community. The apostle Paul admonishes us to bear one another's burdens. This does not mean you are supposed to fix the problems of others, but you are advised to find a spiritual friend, pastor, or counselor to journey with you as you cope with the pain of grieving. The supportive person is there primarily to help the mourner discover his or her pathway for growth and healing.

People experience more losses and crises as they grow older. When you have a good support system, you will be better prepared to cope with pain and loss. Healthy relationships should serve as resources to help you choose holistic ways to move through pain and sorrow.

If you have God in your life, you will cope better, even when the source of your pain and grief cannot be changed. Your connection with the divine and others provide inner strength and a hopeful future to keep you moving toward health and wholeness.

Who do you turn to when you are faced with an emotional crisis of loss? What things do you put your hope in? Remember these two biblical truths: You are not alone, and troubles don't last forever. Peter puts it this way:

"And after you have suffered for a little while, the God of all grace, who has called you to his eternal glory in Christ, will himself restore, support, strengthen, and establish you. " (1 Peter 5:10 NRSV).

Get out your dancing shoes! It's time to shout and dance, and have a halleluiah time!

REFLECTIONS

THE WIDENESS OF GOD'S LOVE

Ephesians 3:16-19

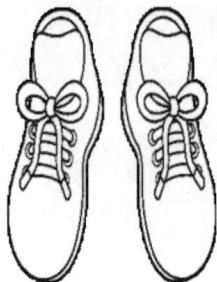

However long you have been under the weight of your grief and pain, there is one thing you can be sure of: "You are not alone." What you are going through is important to God. He wants to give you wings to soar above the valley of pain and loss. Don't lose hope, and don't throw in the towel. *"God is our refuge and strength, a very present help in trouble"* (Ps. 46:1 NKJV).

Jesus is your way-maker. He promised never to leave you. Give him your pain and losses. God's love knows no bounds. *"And may you have the power to understand, as all God's people should, how wide, how long, how high, and how deep his love is. May you experience the love of Christ, though it is too great to understand fully. Then you will be made complete with all the fullness of life and power that comes from God"* (Eph. 3:18-19 NLT).

Never forget! Jesus understands what you are going through.

- Jesus knows grief over the loss of a friend or loved one. He mourned the death of his friend, Lazarus, and even wept for him.
- Jesus knows pain. He was beaten almost to the point of death and was crucified on a cross for the world's sins.
- Jesus knows rejection. He was rejected by the very people he came to save.
- Jesus knows loneliness. He was abandoned by his friends, dragged through the courts, and sentenced to be crucified.
- Jesus knows death. He died for the sins of the world.

God is more interested in what is now possible for you than a rehash of the past. Bring all your insufficiencies to the all-sufficient Christ. Come to the compassionate one and leave your burdens there. Remember, God can turn your mourning into joy!

REFLECTIONS

STRENGTH TO THE WEARY

(Isaiah 40:28-31)

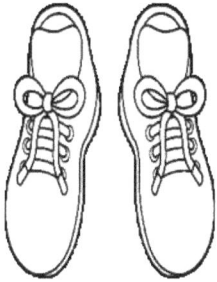

Do you know that God is available to us twenty-four/seven? You may not have given God much thought. You may not believe in God or see any need for God. Even if that's the case, God knows you. He knows your name and even the number of hairs on your head. God saw you being formed in your mother's womb. You owe your existence to God. You were in God's mind before the world existed.

You are important to God. Everything about you and what you are going through matters to God. God created you out of love for his purposes. He is patiently waiting for you to seek to know your Creator, to connect with God. Those who have this connection realize that God's power and strength are available to them in their hour of need. When you are ready, God will be waiting with open arms and acceptance.

"He gives power to the faint and strengthens the powerless. Even youths will faint and be weary, and the young will fall exhausted, but those who wait for the Lord shall renew their strength, they shall mount up with wings like eagles, they shall run and not be weary, they shall walk and not faint" (Isaiah 40:29-31).

Let Isaiah's message remind you why you need to know the one true God who can strengthen and empower you amid your sorrow and loss. As you think about these verses, what words or phrases capture your attention? How do they speak to your current situation?

God is there for you, ready to help shoulder your burdens. Use this occasion to open your heart and mind to the Creator who loves and cares for you. With God in your life, you are never alone as you go through the valley of grief and loss. God is just a prayer away. God wants to give strength to the weary. Don't miss God's best for your life. Allow God's word to strengthen you, giving you wings to rise above your grief and loss, and— dance, dance, dance!

REFLECTIONS

25

Conquering Depression

GOD'S BEAUTIFUL CREATION

Psalm 139:13-16

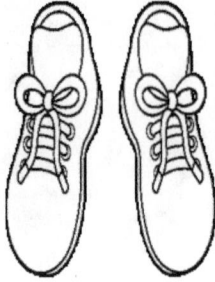

Did you know that God's creation has therapeutic benefits? God created the earth and everything in it for your pleasure, enjoyment, and well-being. A beautiful sunrise or sunset can be breathtaking, releasing certain hormones in the brain that give you joy and a sense of well-being. Observing nature's beauty and magnificent wonders also releases tension in the human body and lift the human spirit. Just being outside in nature can lower your blood pressure and release stress within you. Nature reveals the presence and goodness of God— God's *shalom*.

When the psalmist thought about God's intimate knowledge of his creation and God's interest in his humanity, he was moved to offer praise and worship of the Creator:

> *"For You formed my inward parts; You covered me in my mother's womb. I will praise You, for I am fearfully and wonderfully made, Marvelous are Your works, And that my soul knows very well. My frame was not hidden from You when I was made in secret And skillfully wrought in the lowest parts of the earth"* (Psalm 139:13-15 *NKJV*).

You can learn from the psalmist that God is personally involved in your day-to-day activities. So, when you and I face grief and loss, God is a real and present help. God knows all about you, the good, the bad, and the ugly, and God still loves and accepts you. When you are at your weakest point, God is there, actively working to bring you through. God wants to be the center of your daily life. God is not there to pick up the carnage of your life but to strengthen, heal, and empower you to overcome-- and win.

God wants you to be an over-comer through Jesus Christ. Remember, bad things happen to good people. We learn this vital lesson firsthand in the book of Job. Job also teaches us the importance of continuing to put our complete trust in God's faithfulness and grace, no matter what comes our way. While God cares about the birds of the air, you and I are much more important to God than birds. We have the assurance that God will provide what we need for the journey. Keep in mind, God is a present help in your time of need.

REFLECTIONS

NEW EVERY MORNING

Lamentations 3:21-23

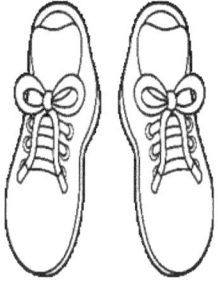

The writer of Lamentations offers us good news, a reminder that you have hope because of God's great love for humanity. God does not deal with you as your sins deserve. God looks at your potential, not your failures, and considers what you can become and not what you are.

The writer of Lamentations gives a revelation of God's enduring characteristic, his compassion and saving grace:

"Because of the LORD's great love, we are not consumed, for his compassions never fail. They are new every morning; great is your faithfulness" (Lam. 3:22-23 NIV).

Knowing about God's love and compassion should not only give you hope day-by-day, but they should compel you to become the best person you can be. God wants you to recognize His presence in your daily life and His compassionate love, and to know that His help and guidance are available to all who trust in Him.

This means that God's people have no reason to whine or complain or question His ability to act decisively concerning your daily needs. God's compassionate love is expressed through his providential care, but his love also demands that you strive to live just and righteous lives before the world.

God still requires his people to face life with courage and hope. If you know, you can depend on God's mercy and goodness—which are new every morning—you can weather any storm, overcome the death of a loved one, and live to His glory and honor in every situation and circumstance!

REFLECTIONS

THE GOOD SHEPHERD

(Psalm 23)

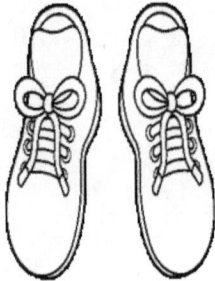

No one is exempt from suffering and evil. Bad things happen to good people, and vice versa. Yet, the psalmist provides assurance that God is there to help those in need, even in the worst of circumstances. God is a loving Shepherd who desires the highest good for his children.

The psalmist declares that God is with you when you go through the valley of the shadow of death. God is near when you feel alone and hopeless. He assures you that he is active in your life, even when you don't recognize His divine presence and interventions.

Because of God's accessibility, you don't have to fear evil. As your loving and compassionate Shepherd, God protects, guides, heals, and delivers you. He promises that death is not the end of life but a transition to more life in the resurrection. The psalmist states:

"Even though I walk through the darkest valley, I will fear no evil,

for you are with me; your rod and your staff, they comfort me" (Psalm 23:4).

If you are walking through a dark place, read the psalmist's words slowly and intentionally. Meditate on their intended meaning. Allow the psalmist's words to flow over you, drawing you closer to the Lord: "he leads me" … "he restores my soul" … "my shepherd" … "quiet waters" … "they comfort me" … "my cup overflows."

Express to the Lord your deepest feelings and emotions. Know that this too will pass. Don't be afraid to bear your soul to the Lord. The Good Shepherd wants to bring you into a spacious place, His sanctuary of grace, peace, and rest.

REFLECTIONS

DEATH AND ETERNAL LIFE

(Luke 23:39-43)

No one will escape death. However, those who put their trust in God's redemptive plan for salvation will receive eternal life. By believing in the saving grace through Jesus Christ, you have the assurance that death is not an end of life but a transition to everlasting life with God.

Luke's narrative of Jesus' crucifixion at Golgotha, with two thieves on each side of him, demonstrates the power of the cross. The crucifixion of Jesus is a historical event, perfectly describing God's providential love, forgiveness, and saving grace, destroying the power of death, changing human history forever.

On Golgotha that day, three men were crucified. One of them knew no sin. Jesus was the sinless Lamb of God who would take away the sins of the world. The two men crucified on each side of Jesus were judged and found guilty of their sins. Jesus asked his Father to forgive those who nailed Him to the cross, for they did not know what they were doing. His death on the cross demonstrated the Father's love for broken humanity. This is why the cross, God's ultimate response to sin, is central to the Christian faith—the good news—the gospel of salvation.

The two thieves nailed on the cross illustrate two opposing responses to the judgment of sin. One of the thieves had an unrepentant heart. He joined those who were hurling insults and mocking Jesus. His attitude matched all those who had rejected Jesus. He chose to remain in his sin condition. Jesus' words of forgiveness went in one ear and out the other.

The other thief acknowledged his sinful condition and confessed his sinfulness to Jesus. With his final breath, he sought God's forgiveness and hopefully asked Jesus to remember him when he would come into his kingdom. He saw in the dying Messiah hope beyond death.

"Then he said to Jesus, *"Lord, remember me when you come into Your kingdom.' And Jesus said to him, "Assuredly, I say to you, today you will be with Me in Paradise"* (Luke 23: 42-43 NKJV).

Jesus told the thief, *"Today, you will be with me in paradise."* Those words are full of meaning. First, they promise that as long as you have breath, forgiveness and eternal life are always possible. Second, they demonstrate that God's love has the power to cover a multitude of sins. Through love, God showed the thief compassion and mercy. Third, Jesus' death on the cross paid the thief's sin debt, including all of humanity. Fourth, you don't have to understand or deserve grace to receive it. Fifth, salvation is a free gift of grace, but it's not cheap.

Jesus gave his life for the salvation of the world. And sixth, salvation must be received by faith through grace.

Three men died that day on Golgotha hill. The thief who turned to Jesus for his salvation was forgiven and went with Jesus to paradise. He will live with God in eternity.[4] The other thief that rejected God's saving grace in Christ Jesus will be forever separated from God. All the people in your life that have died and transition to heaven will live again in the resurrection. You will see them again when you join them in heaven. That is the good news of the kingdom of God. With this hope of seeing your beloved departed, live your life fully in Jesus Christ.

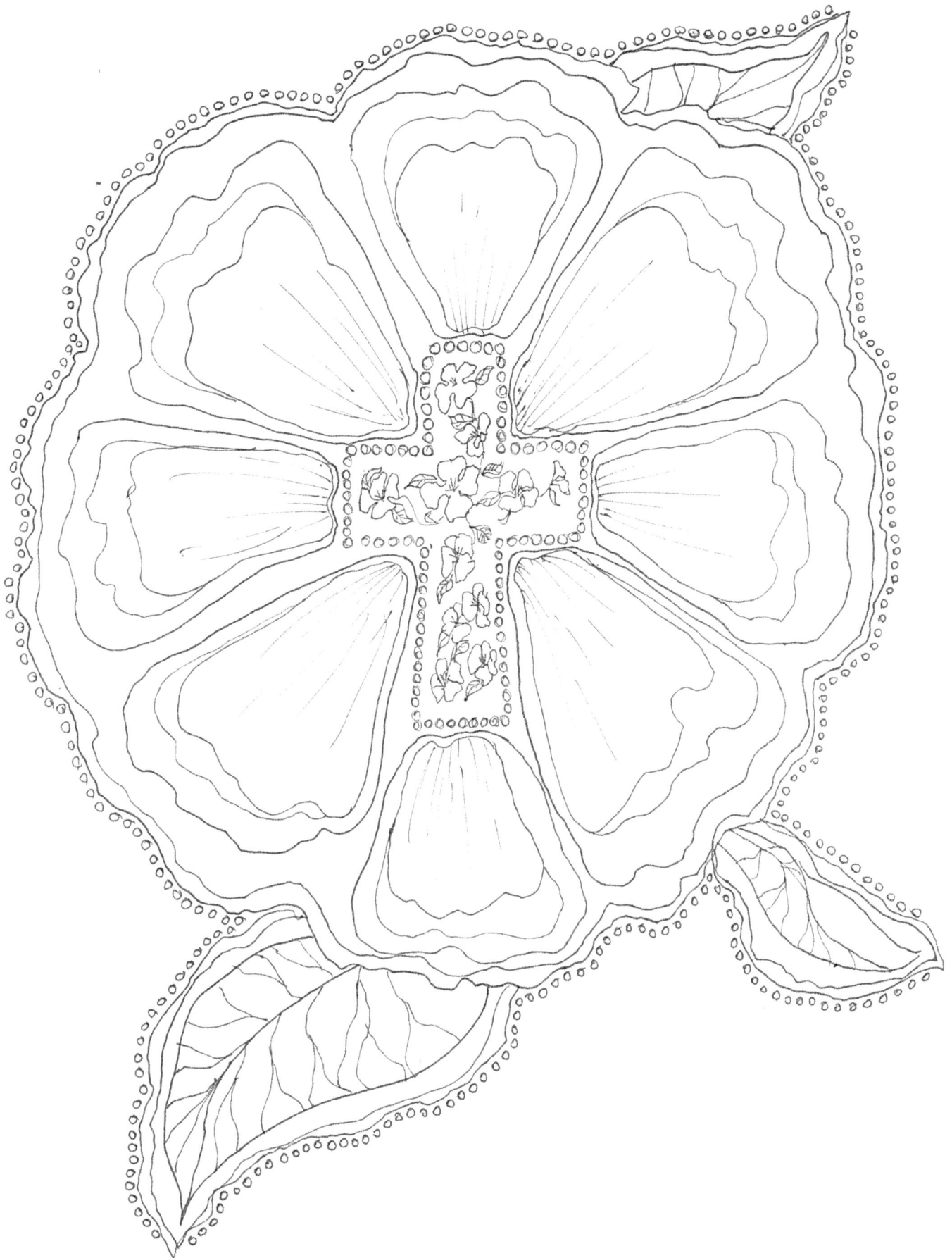

DEATH AND RESURRECTION MADE SIMPLE

(1 Corinthians 15:35-58; John 11:25-26)

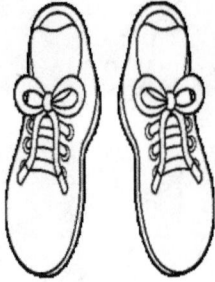

Life is a beautiful thing. As you observe the metamorphosis of a butterfly, you also discover that the new life with Christ is also beautiful. Metamorphosis means change. The New Testament teaches that death is a transition to more life—eternal life. In death, we are transformed into the likeness of Jesus Christ.

The butterfly can only develop by going through all the stages of metamorphosis. The fuzzy caterpillar spins a cocoon in which it rests and develops. When all the changes have taken place, and the butterfly emerges from the cocoon, it is transformed. The opening it makes in the cocoon is a doorway to new life. Without going through the door of death, we cannot receive our new, indestructible bodies.

People who have suffered illness or disabilities for much of their lives will be healed in the resurrection. They will never suffer again. This new, eternal life comes as the result of Jesus' death and resurrection. If we trust God's Son for our salvation, there is no fear of death because God's perfect love removes all fear.

Jesus summed up the meaning of death and resurrection in this way:
"I am the one who raises the dead to life! Everyone who has faith in me will live, even if they die. And everyone who lives because of faith in me will never really die" (John 11:25-26, CEV).

REFLECTIONS

GRACE IN THE MIDST OF GRIEF

Revelations 21:4

Your loved one has passed through the veil to be with the Lord. You feel hurt and angry. Your emotions are tied into knots, and you feel drained. You've asked the questions: Why did my loved one have to die? She was a good person who never did anything wrong or hurt anyone. How will I make it alone? She was my world!

People experience grief differently. Grief does not occur linearly. People don't always start the grieving process in the same way or at the same place. However, shock may be a familiar place that most people experience grief. You may also experience denial and anger in grief. You feel God has let you down. Sometimes you are angry at yourself, perhaps because you wrongly believe something you could have done to prevent your loved one's death. Anger is a handy coping method. But we must not remain in that negative place.

We express anger in four ways. Three of the four expressions—aggressive, passive-aggressive, and suppressive—are unhealthy. Assertive anger is healthy because it moves you toward wellness.[5]

If you are stuck in anger toward the person who died, or God, or yourself, you are in a vulnerable and unhealthy place, but you don't have to remain there. In your state of anger, you don't consider that there is always grace in the midst of grief. Life and death are God's domain alone. God's grace empowers you to let go of your anger and allow Him to transform it into acceptance and peace. You can know that God's grace is at work when you take the step to accept the reality of death.

Next, allow grace to work by telling someone what you are feeling. Permit yourself to express your feelings and emotions freely. Crying is good for the soul. Tears are not only expressions of your feelings and emotions but also an affirmation of your love and longing for that loved one. The more you hurt and mourn, the deeper your love is for the deceased.

Stay connected with family and friends, including your pastor. Connected people mourn better and heal quicker. As you talk about your pain and love for that person, eventually God will turn your mourning into dancing. You will begin moving from anger and denial to acceptance. Mourning gives expression to your grief. Spend time remembering your life with your loved one. Open your eyes to the ways God's grace is working. A time will come when the memory of your loved one won't hurt so much.

God knows how you feel and what you are going through. Tell God all about your troubles. Remember, God is an ever-present help in the time of trouble. John the Revelator reminds us:

"And God will wipe away every tear from their eyes; there shall be no more death, nor sorrow, nor crying. There shall be no more pain, for the former things have passed away" (Rev. 21:4). God wants to turn your mourning into dancing, so keep your dancing shoes nearby!

REFLECTIONS

WE DON'T ALL GRIEVE THE SAME

Scripture

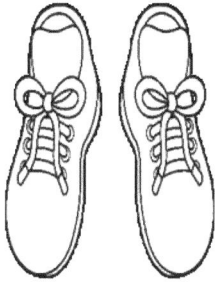

When you experience death or some other significant loss, the first thing you experience is a *shock*. You cannot believe that this could happen to you. Why would a loving God take your loved one? Why would three young children have to lose a parent? Where is the sense in this, you wonder? You have entered an unbelievable, unthinkable nightmare, something that can't be happening. In this state of shock, you become confused and numb. The functions of your body and your mind slow down because you cannot process the sudden stress and the reality of the situation.

A shock is a form of disbelief when the reality is distorted for a short period. The numbness, too, is a short-term safety mechanism to protect you from becoming emotionally overloaded.

This safety mechanism is God's grace working. James L. Mayfield, author of *Discovering Grace in Grief,* points out that grace is a part of every stage of grief. The presence of grace is a reminder that God is not indifferent to human loss and stress. As you open yourself to God, you will discover that he is near, ready to strengthen and help you through any crisis, large or small.

The stages of grief are part of a natural process to help you move toward wellness, even amid loss. Grace informs you that God is an active part of your history, and all human history. God wants you to be well. When God is at the center of your life, in both the good and bad times, you can know you have "*a friend who sticks closer than a brother"* (Prov. 18:24 NKJV).

God has unlimited resources and time to meet you at the point of your need. Turn to the one who loves you and desires your highest good. God has built into your DNA the potential to live an abundant life in Christ. God wants to journey with you through the grief process. Don't stop, and don't give up. God's grace empowers you to move from loss and pain to victory and wellness.

Disclaimer: People experience grief differently or not at all. Grief does not occur linearly. People don't always begin the grieving process in the same way or at the same place. Love is a crucial factor in how a person might experience grief. Grief is a natural part of the growth and healing process.[4]

REFLECTIONS

DENIAL

Luke 24:13-53

Many of Jesus' disciples struggled with accepting his teaching and the scriptural evidence of his death and resurrection. They were in denial. Denial can be a good thing during the initial stage of grief. This phase of grief serves as a protective mechanism to help you deal with extreme stress that the crisis or the death of a loved one has plunged you into. During the short-term state of denial, you may act as if nothing has happened. Also, you may not consider what you hear or see as being real. You may carry on your daily activities as if all is normal, completely unaware of the reality of your crisis. Time may seem to slow down to a pace that allows you to wrap your mind around the reality of what has just happened, keeping you from becoming overloaded emotionally. Denial protects you from experiencing more stress and pain. It is a safe place.[6]

If you can only speak of the deceased person with words or phrases like *passed, passed away*, or *gone to be with the Lord*, you are probably still in denial Words such as *dead, died*, or *deceased* are too painful to say, and you continue to speak of the deceased person in the present tense.[7]

Job is the first person to suggests that life is often not fair or just (See Job 16:3-20.) In every crisis, there are two potentials: danger and opportunity. If you have gone through a crisis, you are aware of the potential for harm due to shattered hopes and deferred dreams. Crises can have a negative impact on your physical and emotional health. If you do not have a personal relationship with God, are not well connected to others, or have a low self-esteem, you most likely won't experience the kind of wellness that could be yours.

Once you accept the reality of the loss, you can see the light of reality and begin life again with hope and a future. This gradual turn to reality offers hope, faith, and love.

Grief has the potential for harm. It can isolate you from loving and caring for people. Pride leads some people to try to work through the grief process on their own, perhaps because others have told them how strong they are. Such pride does more harm than good. When you go through a severe crisis, pride becomes a liability. Pride prevents you from sharing your deep pain and sadness. Pride also keeps you from crying because you must continue to prove that you are strong and in charge of your emotions. Such lies can take you down the path to real harm and emotional destruction.

Never try to hide your grief. Never go through grief in isolation. And never lie to yourself and others. You grieve best in the context of community. God's people are called to "bear one another's burdens" (Gal. 6:2). You are your brothers' and sisters' keeper. Do not treat denial as a dysfunction, but allow it to complete its purpose so you can be whole once you are on the other side of your grief.

REFLECTION

"COME UNTO ME"

Matthew 11:28-29

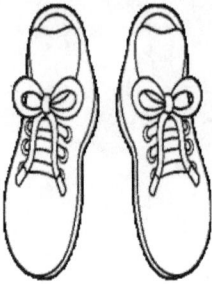

Whether you are coming out of your crisis or you are stuck in the valley of despair, Jesus is calling, "Come unto me." Jesus' call is personal and significant. It is personal because Jesus came "to proclaim liberty to the captives" (Luke 4:18). Jesus is keenly aware that much of what you are going through comes from an invisible and incapacitating foe, called stress. Jesus' call is significant because you were designed for peace, not for stress.

In *Discovering Grace Grief*, James Mayfield reminds us that there is an emotional storm within the grief process:

> *"It happens when we realize how much we miss the person who is dead. It happens when we begin to sense how much we will miss the person in the future. It happens when we realize that some hopes and dreams we had related to that person will never be fulfilled. It happens when it dawns on us that a person who has been a vital part of our lives is now only a memory for us."[8] Stress can be a silent and misunderstood killer. In our culture, we often try to deny or hide the emotional storm of grief. We believe happiness is good, but sadness is bad. Because of this attitude, you may be tempted to pretend you are not sad; sadness is bad; consequently, you don't grieve well.*

Holding in your sorrow and sadness overloads you emotionally. If you have observed a boiling teapot, you know the importance of releasing the pressure of the boiling water. In the same way, you must release the inner tension of grief by expressing your true feelings and emotions, first to God and to those with whom you have a strong relationship.

Jesus is aware of the complexities of human nature and the danger in your crises and losses. In the full text of this verse, he says,

> *"Come to me, all you who are weary and burdened, and I will give you rest. Take my yoke upon you and learn from me, for I am gentle and humble in heart, and you will find rest for your souls. For my yoke is easy and my burden is light"* (Matt. 11:28-29 TLB).

When you take on his yoke, Jesus becomes your strength, your support, and your peace for the journey. He helps you to become aware of your inner strength given by the Holy Spirit. The Holy Spirit strengthens you in your weakness and helps you learn how to heal and grow through crises and losses.

Jesus reminds you that in him, you can bear fruit in your day-to-day challenges. Jesus calls you to come to him and to rest in his presence. You are told to abide in him as a branch must abide in the vine, if you are to bear fruit that lasts. Not only are you to abide in him, but also to abide in God's Word, as a source of life and strength.

REFLECTIONS

GROWING THROUGH GRIEF

2 Corinthians 12:7-10

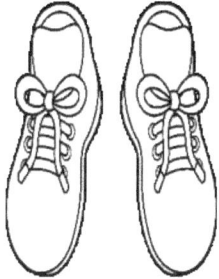

As you go through the grieving process, you will know you are in trouble when you find yourself stuck. Your sadness leads to stress; stress turns into hopelessness; hopelessness results in depression. Depression is accompanied by feelings of worthlessness and even thoughts of suicide. If this is your reality, seek immediate medical intervention, as well as spiritual counseling.

Remember, grief is a natural process typical to everyone who has experienced a significant loss. However, grief does not have to end badly. When the grief work is done well, it has the potential to make you stronger, wiser, and more compassionate toward others who are going through the stress of pain and loss.

In his book, *Anchoring Your Well Being*, the late Howard Clinebell, Ph.D., lists six strategies that can help you heal and grow through grief.

Task 1. Gradually let go of denial and accept the painful reality that your loss has occurred. Denial is a gift from God to protect your mind from being overwhelmed until you can slowly take in the devastating facts. Keep on moving forward, not forgetting that God created you to be a whole person, no matter what life throws at you. You are created in God's image and for greatness.

Task 2. Allow yourself to experience the full range of your feelings and emotions. The key is not to repress your emotions and painful feelings. There is always a brighter side to life. God will help you figure it all out, but you must stay in the game.

Task 3. Take precautions in decision-making during the early stages of the grieving process. Seek out wise counsel as you navigate through this stressful time.

Task 4. Put your life back together step by step. You must make peace with your past and with those who have hurt or left you.

Task 5. Evaluate and stretch your faith as you accept and embrace your new future. Strive to find meaning and purpose in every stage of life.

Task 6. Use your experience of going through the grief process to help others benefit from what you have learned. Hurting people need to know that God is both present and faithful in times of pain and loss. Your grief work can be invaluable in ministering to others. God has blessed you to be a blessing to others. God called and blessed Abraham to bless all the people of the world who would enter

into the covenant God made with him. God said:
> *"I will make you into a great nation. I will bless you and make you famous, and you will be a blessing to others. I will bless those who bless you and curse those who treat you with contempt. All the families on earth will be blessed through you"* (Gen. 12:2 NLT).

REFLECTIONS

ENDNOTES

1. Martinez, Nikki, Psy.D., LCPC. Huffpost: 7-Reasons Adult Coloring Books Are Great For Your Mental, Emotional And Intellectual Health

2. This special song, *In Your Presence* was written by Gloria Jean Parker Penn. © 2009. Used with permission.

3. This special poem was written by Willie Mae Crump, a gifted writer, author, friend, and fellow church member. I am grateful to her for allowing the use of her poem in this book. Crump created this special poem for a new ministry called A New Season. This ministry was designed by Reverend Renata Williams to help support persons who have experienced the death of a loved one or friend. The New Season ministry is offered on a regular basis to comfort and support the grieving community and to experience hope, spiritual growth, and healing. This ministry is in its third year at Allen Temple A.M.E. Church in Woodstock, GA. Used with permission.

4. A note about paradise. Paradise was the holding place for the righteous dead prior to the resurrection of Jesus. After Jesus' resurrection, those held in paradise were released to enter the presence of God. All who die trusting in Jesus as their Savior, enter God's holy presence. Those who reject God's plan of saving grace through Jesus enter hell when they die. Jesus revealed this truth in the story about the deaths of the rich man and Lazarus. The rich man ends up in hell, and Lazarus goes to heaven. Paradise is now empty and no longer exists.

5. Adapted from *The Angry Smile: The Psychology of Passive-Aggressive Behavior in Families, Schools, and Workplaces, 2nd Ed. (pp. 9-12), by J. E. Long & S. Whitson, 2009, Austin, TX: PROED.* © 2009 by PRO-ED, Inc. Adapted with permission.

6. Axelrod, Julie. (2017). The 5 Stages of Grief & Loss. *Psych Central.* Retrieved on August 11, 2017, from https://psychcentral.com/lib/the-5-stages-of-loss-and-grief/

7. Mayfield L., James. Discovering Grace In Grief. Nashville: Upper Room Books, 1994. (p.31).

ABOUT THE AUTHORS

Dr. John I. Penn is a retired ordained United Methodist minister. From 2002 to 2008, Penn served as the pastor of Simpson United Methodist Church in Wilmington, Delaware. Before coming to Simpson, he served seven and a half years, as the Director of Spiritual Formation and Healing at Upper Room Ministries. As an ordained minister, he has served several pastorates in the Peninsula-Delaware Annual Conference. He has served the church for over thirty years. Penn has served in two cross-racial appointments as the associate pastor.

Penn is a native of Roanoke, Virginia. He is the author of several books: *Rediscovering Our Spiritual Gifts* (Upper Room Books), a companion workbook for Dr. Charles Bryant's book of the same title; *Getting Well, A Study for Children about Spiritual and Physical Healing* (originally published by Abingdon Press); *Equipped to Serve, A Study for Children about the Gifts of the Holy Spirit*, and *About Caring and Healing, An Activities and Coloring Book for Children*. He has recently published his new book, *Miracles of Healing in the Gospel of Mark*. Penn has completed the writing of a Leader's Guide for *Miracles of Healing of the Gospel of Mark,* which will be published in 2021. He has also written booklets for youth and children: *What Everyone Should Know about Healing* (Companion to *About Caring and Healing*); *Understanding the Gifts of the Holy Spirit*; and *About the Gifts of the Holy Spirit.*

Penn is married to Gloria J. Parker Penn. They have six children (one deceased), ten grandchildren, and three great-grandchildren. He loves to write, compose music, listening to jazz, gardening, and teaching tennis.

Wanda Shoemaker Parker Rains was born in Knoxville, TN where she received a BFA from the University of TN. She has lived in several states and Africa. She has had a variety of artist positions; among them are illustrating and drafting for engineering and planning firms, on the art staff of a sign company, a newspaper and a printing company, and has worked as a contract and freelance artist. Wanda and her husband, John, now live in New Bern, NC.

Wanda has a personal understanding of grief having lost her first husband to suicide and her sister to a rare disease. Her drawings are an attempt to express some of her feelings during those painful times and the growth that came through the process.